The J.J. Donovan

Treasures From The Trunk

Whatcom Museum

Presenting Sponsor
Sanitary Service Company

Supporting Sponsors
Nielsen Brothers Inc.
Steve & Neelie Nelson
The Donovan Family
Rotary Club of Bellingham

by
Brian L. Griffin

Museum catalog for
Treasures from the Trunk, The J.J. Donovan Story
Copyright © 2013 Knox Cellars Publishing Company

ISBN: 978-0-9635841-6-8

Published in conjunction with the 2013 exhibition
Treasures from the Trunk, The J.J. Donovan Story
organized by
Whatcom Museum
121 Prospect Street, Bellingham, Washington
360.778.8930

Photographic assistance: Jeffrey Jewell
Editorial assistance: Gayle Helgoe
Catalog design and production: Kate Weisel, weiselcreative.com
Printed in the United States of America

Front cover image: John Joseph Donovan, printed from an antique printing plate; and his diary, both found among the treasures from the trunk. Back cover photo is the trunk itself.

Notice to historians and researchers:
The contents of 'The Trunk' described in this catalog will be available for research at the Center for Pacific Northwest Studies, a unit of the Division of Heritage Resources, Goltz-Murray Archives Building, Western Washington University, 808 25th Street, Bellingham Washington, 98225-7747 ph: 360.650.7747 email: cpnws@wwu.edu

Director's Foreword

The Whatcom Museum is pleased to present **Treasures from the Trunk: The J.J. Donovan Story** as told by our guest curator, Brian Griffin. When the idea for the exhibition was presented to me by Brian some one and a half years ago, a major focus was the discovery of a statue in Bellevue that had been given by J.J. Donovan in 1928 to St. Joseph's Hospital in Bellingham in memory of his young grandsons.

The statue was found by Brian at a Catholic convent in Bellevue and his goal was to attempt to bring it to the Whatcom Museum as a centerpiece to the exhibition and ultimately to return it to Peace Heath St. Joseph Medical Center to which it had been given all those years before. An ambitious idea, with implications far beyond traditional exhibition curation, but such ideas come with the territory when working with someone like Brian, I was to learn.

We assembled a team of staff to work with him on the project and research continued for many months, largely conducted by Brian who traveled extensively following leads and looking for existing family members who might remember or have anything pertinent to contribute.

Not only did Brian discover many Donovan relations in numerous states, but in an old trunk in the possession of an individual with family ties in Sag Harbor, New York, he found a gold mine of important material that enriched the content of the exhibit in important ways. Fantastic photos, movies, artifacts, and many, many hand-written diaries and letters that add immensely to the historical record of Whatcom County and will enrich the community archives immeasurably.

For the first time in years, the Whatcom Museum will showcase the story of an important historical individual and his contributions. His life story is in many ways the story of the early development of the city of Bellingham and many important industries in the Whatcom County region and beyond.

We are indebted to Brian for the countless hours devoted toward the development of the exhibition and most especially for his amazing gift of raising funds necessary to implement the entire project.

I am especially proud that the exhibit story is documented in this important catalog written by Brian that will live long after the exhibit closes.

Special thanks also goes to the Museum's Photo Archivist/Historian, Jeff Jewell, who is not only incredibly knowledgeable and an excellent historian, but whose talents were invaluable in the exhibit development process. Additionally, the work of Exhibit Designer Scott Wallin and Preparator David Miller deserve special thanks for their wonderful creativity and hard work.

Finally, I wish to give huge appreciation to Paul Razore of Sanitary Service Co. for being the lead sponsor of this exhibition, and to supporting sponsors Steve and Neelie Nelson, Nielsen Brothers Inc., The Rotary Club of Bellingham, and members of the Donovan family.

Patricia Leach, Museum Director

An Archivist's Perspective

Delving into it, the contents of the trunk are the stuff of a researcher's dream! For a historian, it is indeed treasure. It's a mother lode of elaborating details and micro-level clues from which discoveries are made and mysteries solved. It's all very exciting and Brian Griffin has been giddy with it.

The treasure found in J.J. Donovan's steamer trunk is nothing less than the man's diaries, business correspondence, personal letters, poetry, and miscellaneous printed materials he collected along the way. In addition to ephemera, there are family photographs and home movies.

It's quite amazing how much material has survived, especially considering the generational and geographical distance the items have traveled. Credit J.J. Donovan's descendants who recognized the value of his papers and saved them, believing that *someday* their value would be appreciated. They had no way of knowing just how long that day would take to arrive. There must have been a certain kind of faith involved.

This exhibition serves as an introduction, a first gleaning of the treasures. Next will be conservation and cataloging at the Center for Pacific Northwest Studies at Western Washington University. From there, accessible to the community, will come interpretations, context, connections, and extractions of exquisite minutiae.

Not only is this collection full of missing pieces to the puzzle, the puzzle itself just got larger. Our picture of J.J. Donovan will come into ever sharper focus as historians work with this material. The collection's bounty is enough to take the past far into the future.

Jeffrey Jewell, Whatcom Museum Archivist/Historian

Introduction & Acknowledgements

JOHN JOSEPH DONOVAN was arguably the most important citizen of the towns surrounding Bellingham Bay during his lifetime. He had arrived on the Bay in 1888 when the population of its four towns aggregated barely four hundred souls. At his death in 1937, the population of Bellingham had exceeded thirty thousand, and the Bellingham Herald mourned the loss of "Bellingham's first citizen". He had done much to earn that praise. His history is very much the history of Bellingham. His story was a story that needed to be told.

The impetus to mount this exhibition honoring him began when the statue of St. Joseph, which had stood for so many years above the State Street entrance to St. Joseph's Hospital, was found on the grounds of St. Mary's on the Lake convent in Bellevue, WA. The realization that Donovan had given it to the hospital in 1928 in memory of two deceased grandsons strengthened our resolve that it should properly be returned to Bellingham, thus igniting the idea for this exhibition.

Seeking relatives to help in asking for the statue's return led to finding 'The Trunk' in Sag Harbor, NY. The trunk contained an extensive collection of thousands of personal and business papers and artifacts from Donovan's fruitful life. Because his life story is also the story of the beginning years of the City, the papers are an invaluable chronicle of the early history of Fairhaven, Bellingham, Whatcom, and Sehome and the consolidated City of Bellingham in its first 35 years.

Treasures from the trunk included 2,047 personal letters beginning in 1872, written by hand and still in their original envelopes. There were 41 of Donovan's personal diaries begun in 1874 and more than a thousand business letters with letterheads from scores of early businesses. The trunk held thousands of snapshots, both negatives and prints, tintypes, photographic printing plates, early 16-mm movies and scores of newspaper clippings relating to Donovan's activities. This historical treasure was saved by the family and is now safeguarded in the archives of the City that J.J. served so well.

We are deeply in debt to Kathy Riggs, great granddaughter of the Donovans and executor of her mother's estate. Her recognition of the importance of the Trunk's contents assured that it would be preserved. She then generously donated its treasures to our archives, knowing that they would be protected and available for scholarly research to future generations.

I owe a personal debt of gratitude to Albert Riggs who carefully stored the Donovan Collection in his home in Sag Harbor for many years and has become a close friend over the months that we have worked together to transport the collection to Bellingham.

My sincere thanks to grandson Donovan Craven and his wife Avery for the loan of important family memorabilia;

Neelie Nelson, who with her remarkable research skills, found relatives, photographs and information that were fundamental in mounting the exhibition;

Jeff Jewell, the Whatcom Museum's Photo Archivist. His deep knowledge of local history has contributed immensely to the exhibition and his professional skills have added greatly to its presentation. It has been a joy to work with him.

And especially my unbounded appreciation goes to Gayle Helgoe, retired librarian, fully engaged historian, who has worked with me for countless hours over the past twelve months as we read thousands of letters, organized the collection, thrilled at our discoveries, wrote captions, and worked at this catalogue. How can I ever thank you enough?

The pursuit of history seems to be a journey with no beginning and no end. This exhibition began with the discovery of a marble statue when on a prior project. The rich life story uncovered among the *Treasures from the Trunk* leads into another project that I plan to write, the biography of this remarkable man, John Joseph Donovan.

In the meantime it is a rare privilege to curate this exhibition. I am grateful to Patricia Leach for the opportunity.

My wish and expectation is that you will enjoy the show, learn a great deal about our city and come away with a profound respect and liking for the man who did so much to build it.

Brian L. Griffin, Guest Curator

Treasures From The Trunk
The J.J. Donovan Story

Like so many American life histories, the J.J. Donovan story begins with the tragedy of the Irish Potato Famine.

In the town of Skibbereen, County Cork, at the very southern tip of Ireland lived Denis and Julia Donovan. Like most of their neighbors, the Donovans were devout Catholics, poor tenant farmers eking out a living for their large family of ten children. Like most Irish peasants of the day, their livelihood depended on the lowly potato.

In the summer of 1845, a fungal blight spread like the shadow of death over all of northern Europe. The potato crop was ruined. Newly dug potatoes dissolved into an inedible watery, putrid mass just hours after they were dug. It was indeed the shadow of death for the poor of Ireland, impacting one million who starved to death or died from diseases that struck the weakened populace. Nowhere in Ireland was the famine or its attendant agonies worse than in Skibbereen. Another million desperate Irish fled the country, crowding onto the "famine ships" taking them to America and elsewhere around the world.

"Skibbereen" by Mahony, 1847

By 1848, the Donovan family had saved enough money for passage to send their 23-year-old son Peter to America. His goal was to work hard and send money home to pay passage for other siblings who would follow. His ticket took him to Boston where he soon secured a job as laborer with the Boston, Concord & Montreal Railroad.

At that time the BC&M was building its track up the western valley of New Hampshire to service the many summer resorts in the White Mountains. Peter was strong, intelligent and hardworking and soon became a foreman. Within two years he was able to send passage money for a brother and sister.

photo courtesy of Ellen Hegeman

Peter Donovan, 1825–1885

COPY of Report and List of the Passengers taken on board the *Ship Plymouth Rock* of *Boston* 1869 whereof *Obed Caldwell* is Master, burthen *472* tons, and *son* of a ton, bound from the Port of *Liverpool* for *Boston*

NAMES.	AGE.	SEX.	Occupation, Trade, or Profession.	Country to which they severally belong.	Country of which they intend to become inhabitants.	Remarks relative to any who may have died or left the vessel during the voyage.
Mary Gilhooly	17	Female		Ireland	U. States	
Ann Cullen	7					
John Malone	50	Male				
Edward Martin	17					
Cecilia McLaughlin	30	F				
Mary Dogan	50					
Thomas	19	M				
Thomas Walsh	29					
Bridget McGrath	7	F				
William Costello	19	M				
Bridget Flynn	17	F				
Bridget Perkins	28					
Thomas Nugent	40	M				
Mary	35	F				
Nicholas	4	M				
Thomas Rourke	38					
Mary Collins	17	F				
Bridget	11					
Mary Barry	18					
Mary Deane	25					
Patrick Donovan	20	M				
Margaret	19	F				
James O'Neil	48	M				
Michael Sullivan	19					
John Hawkes	22					
Jane McBrien	15	F				
Roxanna Stearns	50					
John	17	M				
Owen Barker	18	M				
Honor Barry	54	F				
James Atherwood	16	M				
Emma	11	F				
Benjamin	9	M				
Thomas Shipley	49		Weaver	England		
Margaret Collins	20	F		Ireland		
Elizabeth McCullagh	50					
Jane Graham	14					
Thomas Long	37	M				
John Collins	14					
Ellen	10	F				
Catherine Brennan	65					

Manifest of the S.S. *Plymouth Rock*

photo courtesy of Ellen Hegeman, descendant of Margaret

photo courtesy of Ellen Hegeman

Margaret Donovan was 19 years old upon her arrival in Boston. In 1859 she met and married Patrick Dulin in Haverhill, Massachusetts. Dulin was a laborer, and they had seven children. Margaret died on January 29, 1896 in Clermont, Iowa.

Patrick Donovan, 1829–1902

Patrick and Margaret Donovan booked passage on the ship *Plymouth Rock*. They arrived in Boston on the 26th of December, 1850. The Donovan family was eventually able to send eight of their children to America in this manner. Patrick, age 20, joined his brother Peter working on the BC&M Railroad. He also began as a laborer and was soon promoted to foreman. Patrick eventually became a 'Section Man', responsible for the maintenance of a section of the completed track.

The hard working Donovan brothers eventually found wives among the hundreds of thousands of Irish immigrants in New England. Peter met and married Julia Whooley, and Patrick Donovan, in 1856 married Julia O'Sullivan.

photo courtesy of Ellen Hegeman

Julia Whooley immigrated with an aunt when she was only 12 years old. In 1846 they left Ireland on a sailing ship. Almost shipwrecked, their ship staggered into Nova Scotia after 17 weeks at sea. They made their way to Boston. She married Peter Donovan on November 4, 1851. He was 29, she was 17. They had six children.

Two years later, when Patrick and Julia were living in Rumney, New Hampshire, their first child arrived. John Joseph Donovan was born on September 8, 1858.

Young Donovan was destined to live a life of achievement and prominence. In many ways his life would typify the 'American Dream'.

Treasures from the Trunk

This tintype is the earliest known photograph of J.J. Donovan. He was the first child of Patrick and Julia Donovan. His age in this picture is estimated at 14 years (c. 1872).

The Boston, Concord & Montreal Railroad (BC&M) was constructed up the western valley of New Hampshire in the 1850s. It operated for many years on the old stage coach route taking summer visitors to the resorts in the White Mountains of northern New Hampshire and serving the towns along the valley all the way to Canada.

He was a child of impoverished immigrants, who by virtue of his will and determination, rose to a position of wealth and influence in an exciting period of American history.

In 1860 Patrick Donovan was appointed Section Man in charge of section 12 of the BC&M Railroad. He was responsible for the 10 or 12 miles of track between Plymouth and Rumney. The Donovans bought a small farm alongside the track about one mile north of Plymouth. They would call Plymouth home for the rest of their lives. Patrick worked for the BC&M for a total of 35 years.

Plymouth Main Street, 1880. The small town of Plymouth was the central town of Grafton County. It was a market town and a center for leather glove manufacturing and leather tanning. It was also the site of the Plymouth Normal School, a training school for teachers.

Young John Donovan thrived in the small town of Plymouth. He developed a healthy social life with friends in the village. When very young he assumed many duties on the farm doing daily chores, tending the chickens, pigs and sheep. He kept goats which he trained to pull a cart. He hunted grouse in the woods, sawed and split firewood, worked the garden, fished and swam in the river and ponds, trapped muskrat and picked copious amounts of berries in season. In early Spring he helped with the maple sugar harvest. His diaries are filled with the joys and responsibilities of an intelligent and adventurous boy of that time.

From the collection of the Plymouth Historical Society, Plymouth, NH

"Birdseye Views" were common promotional pieces in the late 19th century. These artists conceptions accurately show each building and feature of a city and are a valuable historic reference to many American cities. This "Birdseye" of Plymouth shows the town as it was the year after J.J. Donovan began his career as a civil engineer. Note the covered bridge across the river, the Normal School, and Pemigewasset House beside the railroad track.

PEMIGEWASSET HOUSE

Plymouth for a time was at the end of the BC&M Railroad line. It was an important way point for the seasonal resort business of the White Mountains. Vacationers would disembark at Plymouth and complete their journey to the resorts via stagecoach. The BC&M built the luxurious Pemigewasset House to accommodate those travelers. The lower floor of the hotel was the train station.

The Plymouth Normal school was established in 1871 and led the nation in teacher training. It was a model for our own Normal School, now Western Washington University.

John Joseph Donovan began keeping meticulous diaries in 1872 at the age of 13. The diaries of his childhood give us an understanding of the adult that he would become. Highly intelligent, sensitive, energetic and ambitious with a wide-ranging curiosity and broad cultural, political and intellectual interests.

After a beginning grammar school education in the one room school houses of the day, young John was able to enroll in the grammar school of the Plymouth Normal School (similar to the former Campus School in Bellingham's Western Washington University). There he excelled in schoolwork and passed from the grammar school to the college itself. He graduated in 1877 at age 17.

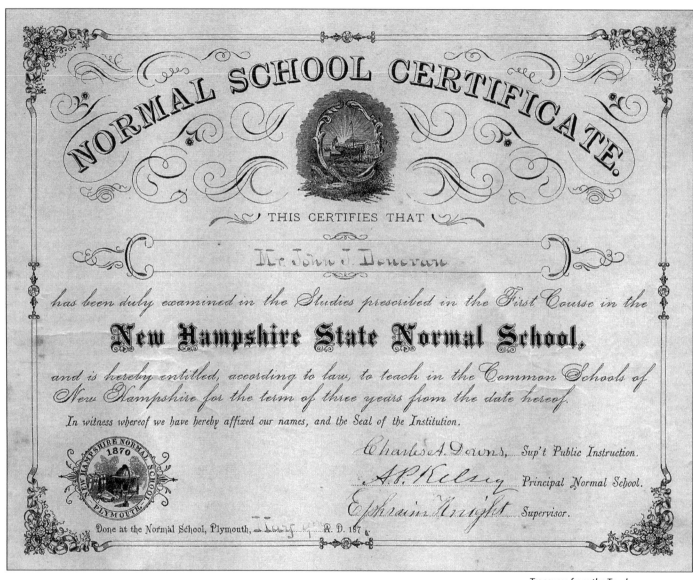

NORMAL SCHOOL CERTIFICATE.

THIS CERTIFIES THAT

Mr. John J. Donovan

has been duly examined in the Studies prescribed in the First Course in the

New Hampshire State Normal School,

and is hereby entitled, according to law, to teach in the Common Schools of New Hampshire for the term of three years from the date hereof.

In witness whereof we have hereby affixed our names, and the Seal of the Institution.

Charles A. Downs, Sup't Public Instruction.

A.P. Kelsey, Principal Normal School.

Ephraim Knight, Supervisor.

Done at the Normal School, Plymouth, ___ A.D. 187_

Treasures from the Trunk

On January 28, 1876, J.J.'s diary records, "…went on the mail train to Lake Village with a group of students. Among them was Clara Nichols." The next day his diary entry was a single capitalized word "NICKIE". He was immediately smitten, but it would be 12 long years before they married.

Treasures from the Trunk

Clara I. Nichols, 'Nickie'

These were 12 years of a relationship threatened by serious differences and large geographic distances. He was the son of Irish immigrants, she a Puritan with roots in American soil reaching back to 1630. Donovan was a devout Catholic, Clara a committed Congregationalist. The letters of the Trunk portray in touching fashion a friendship growing to affection which finally blossomed into a love that could not be denied.

Clara was born and raised in Haverhill, New Hampshire, and was a fine musician and pianist.

Typical of the one room schools of the day, this is the Beech Hill School in Plymouth, NH, c.1890. Clara taught here for one term. She had 26 students.

Both J.J. and Clara graduated in the class of 1877. They successfully passed their teaching examinations and soon were each teaching in one-room village school houses. J.J. taught in Littleton, NH. Only 17 years of age, his class consisted of 24 students whose ages ranged from age 5 to age 19, the eldest student older than the teacher.

Both J.J. and Clara wearied of school teaching after three years. J.J. was determined to become a civil engineer. Clara moved to Melrose, Massachusetts, where she became a piano teacher.

Treasures from the Trunk

This photo of Donovan has written on its back, in his handwriting, "at 21". In a letter from Nickie dated Feb. 20, 1880, she writes, "Thank you ever so much for that photo John, it is a splendid one, I think, with all due respect to Kate's opinion. Take good care of that mustache John and in no evil moment give it a death shave."

Treasures from the Trunk

J.J.'s ultimate goal was to become a civil engineer. With encouragement and some financial aid from an uncle, he enrolled in Worcester Polytechnic Institute in Massachusetts. He graduated with the class of 1882. He was elected Valedictorian.

Immediately after graduation he was hired by the Northern Pacific Railroad that was building its transcontinental track across the northern plains. His great adventure in the wilds of the West began.

Boynton Hall, Worcester Polytechnic Institute, Worcester, MA.

This family portrait was taken by a Plymouth photographer on July 14th, 1882, the day before J.J. left for the West. His diary of that day reads as follows, "Had my life insured for $1,000 payable to Father. Bought a five-shot Colts revolver and made general preparations for starting west. Mame came down from Profile House this noon and we all sat for a family picture at the photographers".

(Back row): John Joseph Donovan, Katherine 'Kate' Donovan, Daniel Donovan. (Front row): sisters Margaret 'Maggie', Julia Teresa 'Tot', and Mary Agnes 'Mame', with Patrick Donovan. Mother, Julia O'Sullivan Donovan had died in 1879.

After graduation, 'Billy' Barlow and Donovan, hired by Northern Pacific, traveled by train to "end of track" at Pompeys Pillar, Montana, then by stagecoach 400 miles further west to Deer Lodge.

Donovan's diary describes the first day of their six-day stagecoach ride across the Plains. "The ride today has been the hardest and most disagreeable that I have ever experienced." Choking clouds of alkali dust, 90-degree heat, ten passengers crowded into the coach made for a difficult trip, but the scenery thrilled them and stopovers in Bozeman and Helena restored them for the final push over the Rockies to Missoula.

For six years Donovan worked in advance of the railroad track, surveying, planning and supervising the building of

Treasures from the Trunk

25th anniversary of the Worcester Polytechnic class with J.Q. 'Billy' Barlow standing third from the left. J.J. Donovan is standing sixth from the left. The year was 1907.

The Montana Historical Society Research Center, Montana Historical Society, Helena, MT

Montana Stagecoach

roadbed and bridges. He lived in tents and log cabins in all kinds of weather. Summer and winter, J.J. and hundreds of workers built the railroad that would ultimately be the first to connect Puget Sound to the rest of the nation.

The Northern Pacific Railroad (NP) received its federal charter in 1864 by an Act of Congress, with the signature of President Abraham Lincoln. The goal was to connect the Great Lakes with Puget Sound across the northern territories. Construction began in 1870, from St. Paul, Minnesota in the East and Kalama, Washington Territory in the West.

Whatcom Museum

"Last Spike"
September 8, 1883

The Montana Historical Society Research Center, Montana Historical Society, Helena, MT

Donovan's 1883 diary tells of riding all night out of the mountains of Montana, through a terrible storm to attend the Last Spike ceremony. This remarkable photograph was found in the archives of the Montana Historical Society. Incredibly, Donovan is identified in front of the shed, standing with folded arms and a large western hat, observing the conversation between the Crow Indians and an unidentified white man.

After 13 years of financial and physical struggle, the two tracks were joined. The "Last Spike" ceremony was held at Gold Creek, Montana Territory, September 8th, 1883. Donovan was 25 years old on this day.

The Last Spike event of 1883 completed the NP line to Ainsworth, WT, where trains were ferried across the Snake River to the track running down the Columbia River to Portland, Kalama and Tacoma.

In 1884 the NP began their Cascade division in order to put a shorter track across the Cascade Mountains to Tacoma via Pasco, Yakima, Ellensburg, and Stampede Pass. The railroad contracted with Nelson Bennett to build the road. J.J. Donovan was the NP engineer in charge.

The Cascade Division began at Pasco where trains were landed after being ferried across the Columbia river from Ainsworth. The rails ran north through Prosser, Yakima and up the Yakima River canyon to Ellensburg.

Franklin County Historical Society

Ainsworth was a railroad town on the north side of the Snake River at the confluence with the Columbia. It was 'end of track' and a supply base for railroad construction. Half the population was Chinese laborers, the other half was comprised of grizzled railroad workers, gamblers, and prostitutes. Murders and violence were common. When the railroad bridge across the Snake was completed in 1855, Ainsworth disappeared and is now remembered only by a stone marker along the river.

Whatcom Museum

Bridge built crossing the Yakima in the Yakima River Canyon.

Yakima River – 2nd Crossing

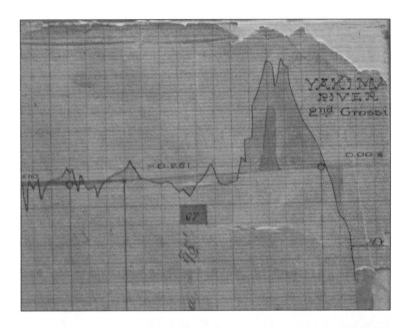

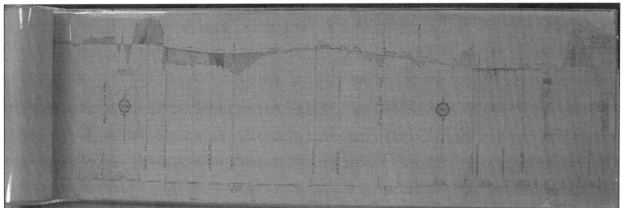

Loaned by Donovan Craven, grandson

This heavy paper scroll was prepared by J.J. Donovan in calculating elevations and grades along the Yakima River. The scroll is 21 feet long and eight inches tall. It is marked in pencil on its outside, "Profile of Yakima Canyon, NPRR. Had charge of construction here, 1855 – J.J.D."

Whatcom Museum

NPRR Engineers' Camp

By May of 1886 the track had been completed on the flat desert lands and up the Yakima canyon to Ellensburgh. Now the engineers entered the rugged and timbered Cascades heading toward Stampede Pass. They lived in tent camps ahead of 'end of track'.

In January 1886, Nelson Bennett won the contract to construct the 9,850-foot tunnel through the mountain crest at Stampede Pass. The tunnel was completed on schedule and on budget on May 3, 1888.

Stampede Tunnel west side. The first train went through on May 27, 1888. The NP track ran down the western slope of the Cascades to Tacoma.

Whatcom Museum

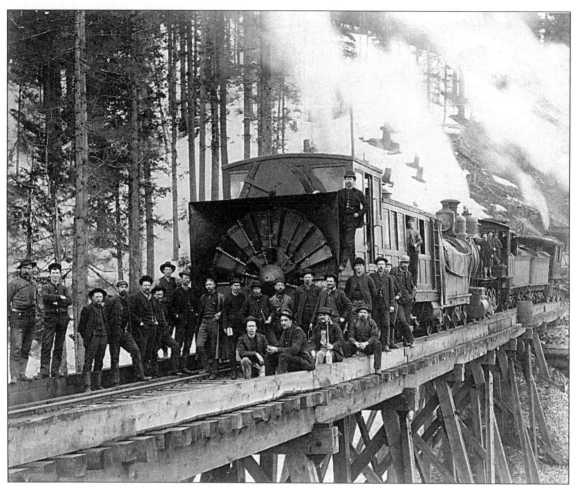

NPRR Snow Bucking Outfit

Heavy snows were a constant challenge during construction. 'Snow bucking outfits' used two rotary snowplows, like this one, facing in opposite directions with four locomotives in between. The strategy kept the plowing unit from becoming trapped if the snow behind became too deep.

Nelson Bennett had been many things—farm worker, oil well driller, land speculator, Indian fighter, mule train operator. Now he was a tough aggressive railroad contractor. He had built the first 135 miles of the Cascade Division from Pasco to Ellensburg, following J.J. Donovan's surveys and engineering plans. He gambled that he could drill the Stampede Tunnel through solid rock on schedule, and he succeeded. He now decided he would be a builder of cities. He bought the town of Fairhaven and created the Fairhaven boom. He needed someone to build a railroad from the town of Sedro to the sea.

Nelson Bennett was impressed with the youthful civil engineer that he had worked with on the Cascade Division contracts.

NELSON BENNETT

Whatcom Museum

Whatcom Museum

On April 6, 1888, Bennett wrote this letter which Donovan received while on his honeymoon.

Bennett had learned from his friend James J. Hill, owner of the Great Northern Railroad, that Hill was bringing his railroad across the Cascades at Sedro on the Skagit River. Calculating that owning the closest deep-water port to Sedro would make him a fortune, Bennett enlisted the financial strength of C.X. Larrabee and together they bought Fairhaven from Daniel 'Dirty Dan' Harris.

He and Bennett also purchased the old town of Bellingham from Eldridge and Bartlett, along with other surrounding properties, combining them all into one much larger Fairhaven.

Whatcom Museum

C.X. Larrabee had amassed great wealth in the copper mines of Butte, Montana, and had increased that fortune in real estate dealings in Portland, Oregon Territory.

Treasures from the Trunk

J.J. Donovan gets a job offer.

Whatcom Museum

onovan accepted Bennett's offer. The job was to design and build a railroad from Sedro to Fairhaven and to develop a coal mine on Bennett's land near Sedro.

J.J. Donovan and his bride Clara rented rooms in Tacoma, and J.J. headed north to Bellingham Bay to survey the railroad route he was to build, start the Cokedale mine,

Fairhaven 1889

This is the earliest photograph of Fairhaven. It appeared on the front page of the Fairhaven Herald, Monday, December 29, 1890, with the caption "Fairhaven, September 1889—population 150". Bennett and Larrabee's plan was working and a year later, September 1890, the population was 7000. The 'boom' was on.

and help with planning the new Fairhaven as the Chief Engineer for the Fairhaven Land Company.

J.J. rode the *Henry Bailey* on June 15, 1888, disembarking at Sterling for his four-day hike to Fairhaven. He was scouting the best railway route for the Fairhaven & Southern RR. Of several possible routes, he chose the Friday Creek, Lake Samish route.

Henry Bailey

The sternwheeler *Henry Bailey* navigated Puget Sound and the Skagit River. A regular route was from Seattle to Utsalady on Camano Island, up the Skagit to Mt. Vernon and then farther upstream to Sterling and Sedro.

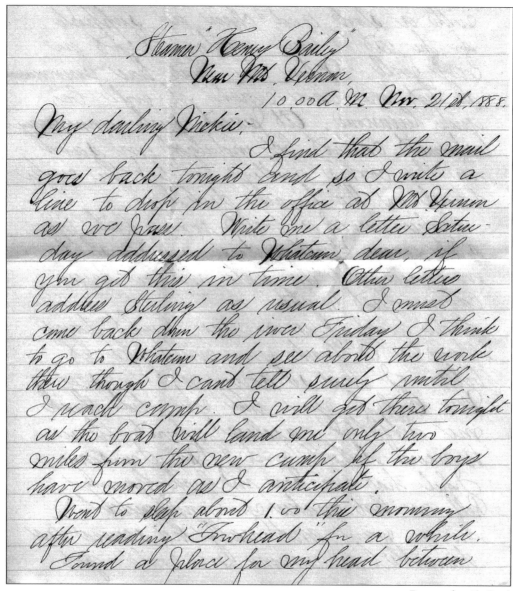

Steamer "Henry Bailey"
Near Mt. Vernon,
10.00 A.M. Nov. 21st, 1888.

My darling Vickie:

I find that the mail goes back tonight and so I write a line to drop in the office at Mt Vernon as we pass. Write me a letter Saturday addressed to Whatcom, dear, if you get this in time. Other letters address Sterling as usual. I must come back down the river Friday I think to go to Whatcom and see about the work there though I cant tell surely until I reach camp. I will get there tonight as the boat will land me only two miles from the new camp if the boys have moved as I anticipate.

Went to sleep about 1.00 this morning after reading "Towhead" for a while. Found a place for my head between

Treasures from the Trunk

Letter written on the *Henry Bailey*. Clara lived in Tacoma for several months while J.J. commuted to his various jobs in Fairhaven. This letter, written on the *Henry Bailey*, describes the accommodations in amusing fashion.

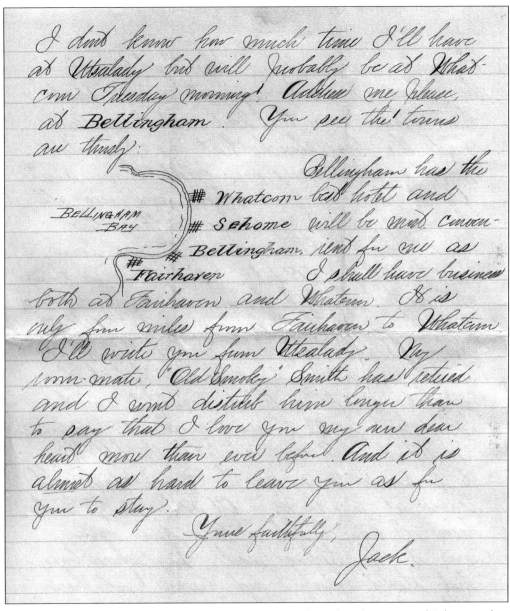

I don't know how much time I'll have at Utsalady but will probably be at Whatcom Tuesday morning. Address me please, at Bellingham. You see the' towns are thusly:

BELLINGHAM BAY

Whatcom
Schome
Bellingham.
Fairhaven

Bellingham has the best hotel and will be most conven-ient for me as I shall have business both at Fairhaven and Whatcom. It is only few miles from Fairhaven to Whatcom. I'll write you from Utsalady. My room-mate, "Old Smoky" Smith has retired and I won't disturb him longer than to say that I love you my own dear heart more than ever before. And it is almost as hard to leave you as for you to stay.

Yours faithfully,

Jack.

Clara was still living in Tacoma. Donovan was planning the railroad. He wrote this letter to her describing the towns around the Bay to which she would soon be moving.

The Bellingham Hotel, 1888

Donovan stayed here when planning the Fairhaven & Southern. It was considered the finest hotel on the Bay in July 1888 when he brought Clara to Fairhaven. They rented rooms here while their house was being built. In an 1888 letter, Clara's pious mother expressed her concern that they lived next to an evil house of sin, probably referring to Monahan's Bar that was then located across the street at 10th & Adams.

Rails for the Fairhaven & Southern

The sailing ship *Charles E. Moody* is unloading steel rails for the new railroad. Donovan designed the dock and supervised its construction in 1889 in his role as Chief Engineer for the Fairhaven Land Company.

The Fairhaven & Southern Railroad to Sedro was completed in 1889. As Chief Engineer for the Fairhaven Land Company, the ever busy Donovan was re-platting Fairhaven. Some streets were renamed to include prominent leaders of the Land Company, and a number of streets were added to the now larger town. Street names included Wilson, Cowgill, Larrabee, and Bennett. Donovan's family is represented by Donovan Avenue and Julia Avenue. His mother's name was Julia and there was a 'Julia' in every generation and branch of J.J.'s family.

Whatcom Museum

Planking Donovan Avenue, 1890

The streets of lower Fairhaven were built over dirt fill. The muddy conditions were best defeated by planking them with boards of the abundant Douglas fir. The Fairhaven City Hall with its small tower can be seen atop the hill in the background.

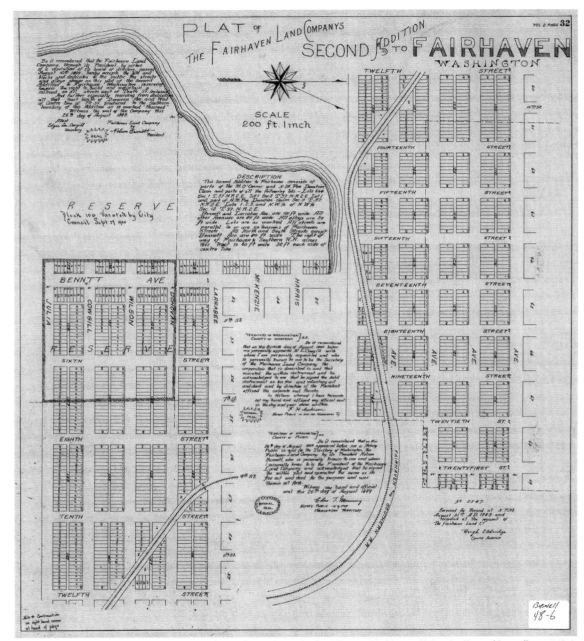

Donovan's Fairhaven Plat, 1889

J.J. Donovan and other notables welcome the first train from Seattle to arrive in Fairhaven over the new Fairhaven & Southern track laid from Sedro, past Lake Samish and across Happy Valley, along Padden Creek to the station at 9th & Harris.

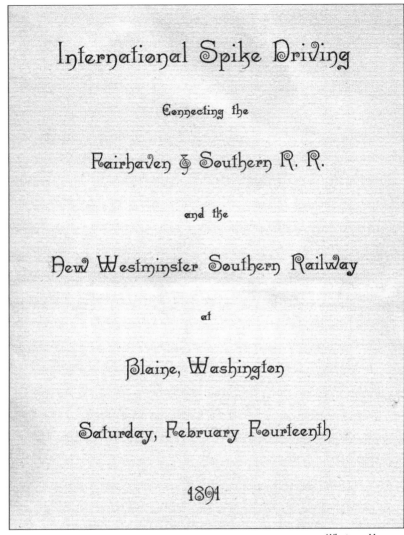

International Spike Driving

Connecting the

Fairhaven & Southern R. R.

and the

New Westminster Southern Railway

at

Blaine, Washington

Saturday, February Fourteenth

1891

The Fairhaven & Southern extends to Canada.

In 1890 the Fairhaven & Southern began its northern extension to Blaine to connect with the Canadian Pacific Railway. Donovan built the track across Bellingham Bay in front of Whatcom on a long trestle. The rails then proceeded north on the right of way still in use. The extension was called the Fairhaven & Northern until 1891 when Bennett and Larrabee sold the entire line to the Great Northern Railway.

J.J. and Clara built themselves a home at 13th and McKenzie in 1889. J.J. was serving his first of two terms on the brand new Fairhaven City Council, and Fairhaven was booming. The huge Fairhaven Hotel was rising on the corner of 12th and Harris. Everyone, including the Donovans, were speculating on Fairhaven lots. Excited investors came from all over the country. Among them was a young man named Julius Bloedel. Bloedel went to work at Jim Wardner's First National Bank of Fairhaven and in a short time became President. He would soon have an important role to play in the life of J.J. Donovan.

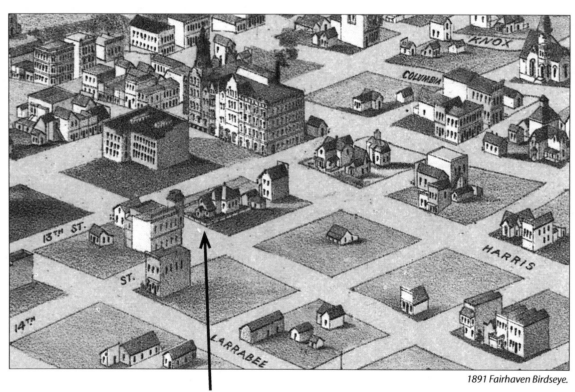

1891 Fairhaven Birdseye.

Donovan home as shown on the 1891 Fairhaven Birdseye.

The Donovan home at 13th and McKenzie

All the Donovan children were born in this house and the Donovans lived here until 1905, when they purchased the house at 1201 Garden Street. This house was demolished in 1968. Apartments now occupy the property at 1301 and 1311 McKenzie.

J. J. DONOVAN

One of the first and most praise-deserving men in the building up of Fairhaven, is that model man, J. J. Donovan, chief engineer of the Fairhaven and Southern railroad. John Joseph Donovan was born Sept. 8, 1858, in Rumney, N. H., of Irish parents who were, as he expresses it, poor but honest and determined that their son should have a better chance in the land of liberty than they had had at

Whatcom Museum

1890 Special Edition
of the Fairhaven Herald.

J.J.'s prominent role in many civic and economic activities resulted in this biographical sketch in a special promotional edition of the Fairhaven Herald of January, 1890.

In 1890, two young nuns were sent to Fairhaven from New Jersey by the Sisters of St. Joseph of Peace. They were directed to establish the first hospital on Bellingham Bay. Sister Teresa Moran and Sister Stanislaus Tighe turned to the most influential Catholic in Fairhaven for assistance. Donovan was able to convince his employers to donate a full city block for the hospital. In addition, he helped them raise money to build it.

Sisters of St. Joseph of Peace Archive

Sister Teresa Moran

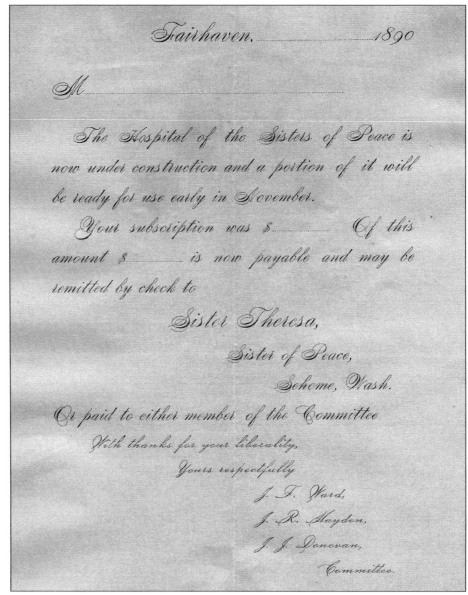

Fairhaven,_____ 1890

M_____

The Hospital of the Sisters of Peace is now under construction and a portion of it will be ready for use early in November.

Your subscription was $_____ Of this amount $_____ is now payable and may be remitted by check to

Sister Theresa,

Sister of Peace,

Sehome, Wash.

Or paid to either member of the Committee

With thanks for your liberality,

Yours respectfully

J. F. Ward,

J. R. Hayden,

J. J. Donovan,

Committee.

Treasures from the Trunk

Donovan and his committee of J.F. Ward and J.R. Hayden solicited cash pledges for the hospital prior to construction. This request for payment was sent to those who had pledged, over the signature of Sister Teresa.

Tacoma, Dec. 10th. 1890

J. J. Donovan Esq.,

      Fairhaven, Wash.,

Dear Sir:-

      Yours of the 8th. inst. from Seattle is at hand. I am
sorry you did not come over to see; your time must be very much
occupied when you cannot spend an extra day to see your old friends.
We are all well here, and are glad to hear that you and yours are
the same.

      With regard to the $500. for the Sister's hospital, you are as
bad as the rest, whenever a man has not got any money you all want
it; at least that seems to be the case. $500. now is as big as a
mountain. I have about $20,000. assessments on different enterprises
in which I am interested that must be paid between now and the first
of the year; and it is going to rustle all the money I can spare.
I fear the Sisters will have to be temporarily put off so far as
Bennett is concerned. Just as soon as I recuperate my finances a
little I will send it to them.

                Yours truly

                Nelson Bennett

Treasures from the Trunk

J.J. solicited his employer Nelson Bennett on behalf of the hospital asking for $500.00 for the construction fund. Bennett was apparently short of cash at the time. This is his response. At least he left open the possibility of a later donation.

St. Joseph's Hospital

The hospital opened in January 1891. It stood on the upper half of the entire block between 16th and 17th Streets, north of Adams Street. Its location is now that of a private residence at 518 17th Street.

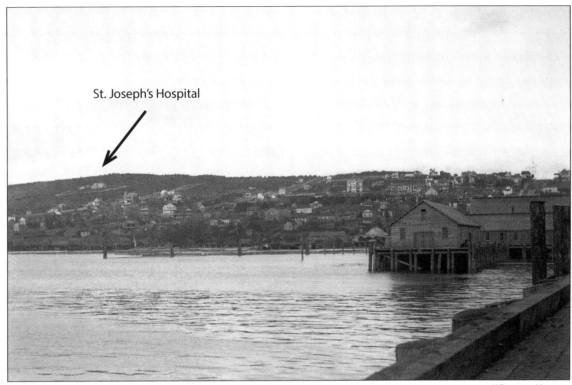

St. Joseph's Hospital

Hospital on the hill, 1892.

This photograph was taken from Ocean Dock. It shows the new hospital surrounded by its white picket fence high on the hill at 17th and Adams. The 14th Street School, replaced by Lowell School in 1914, is visible; as are the Gamwell house, Bateman house and Wardner's 'Castle'.

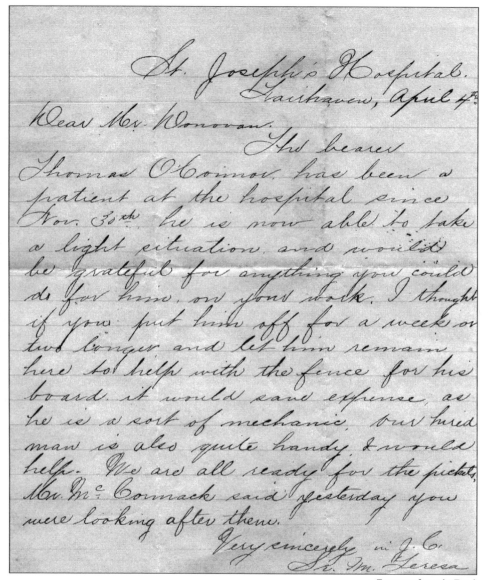

St. Joseph's Hospital.
Fairhaven, April 4th

Dear Mr. Donovan.

The bearer Thomas O'Connor, has been a patient at the hospital since Nov. 30th, he is now able to take a light situation, and would be grateful for anything you could do for him, on your work. I thought if you put him off for a week or two longer and let him remain here to help with the fence for his board, it would save expense, as he is a sort of mechanic, our hired man is also quite handy, & would help. We are all ready for the pickets, Mr. McCormack said yesterday you were looking after them.

Very sincerely in J. C.
Sr. M. Teresa

In this 1891 letter, Sister Teresa gently reminds J.J. that he was "looking after" the pickets, those very pickets shown in the photograph taken from the dock.

The original hospital high on the hill was difficult to access. By 1900, consolidation of Whatcom and Fairhaven was being discussed. A trolley line was running on State Street. The decision was made to abandon the old hospital and build again on Elk Street (State) close to the border between the two towns and on the trolley line. The new building was completed in 1901 and St. Joseph's would remain at that location until 1966.

The Hospital on State Street

As the city grew, more hospital space was needed. A large south wing was added to the building in 1910.

The Compton Addition

By 1928, further space was needed at St. Joseph's Hospital. A major brick addition was built to the north of the original building. It included an elevator and tunnel providing easy access to the State Street level and the streetcar line.

Digging the tunnel.

The Harlow Hollingsworth Funeral Home also ran an ambulance service. The ambulance is seen here in front of the entrance tunnel on State Street.

Whatcom Museum, Jack Carver photo

St. Joseph's Hospital, 1950. The last expansion to St. Joseph's Hospital, a five-story addition on the north side, was completed in October 1950. The $700,000 building added thirty-five beds, new surgeries, labor rooms, nursery, physiotherapy rooms and classrooms for hospitalized children. Unable to expand further at the State Street location, a new 81-bed St. Joseph's Hospital opened in 1966 at the north end of Ellis Street, today's PeaceHeath St. Joseph Medical Center. Parts of the old hospital, including the 1950 expansion and 1927 Compton Pavilion, have since been converted into apartments.

JOHN JOSEPH DONOVAN, long a supporter and advisor to the hospital, commissioned a Carrara marble statue of St. Joseph holding the baby Jesus. The statue, carved in Italy by the noted sculptor, Palla, created a stir when it arrived in Seattle in 1928. It was on display there for a short period and then shipped to Bellingham to be placed atop the new tunnel entrance as a memorial to the two Donovan grandsons who had died in childhood. Philip Hart Donovan died as an infant in his first year of life. John Nichols Donovan Jr., the first Donovan grandchild, died in a tragic automobile accident at age three.

A bronze plaque on the wall
under the Donovan statue was inscribed:

Suffer the children
To come unto me
—
John Nichols Donovan Jr.
1916-1919

Philip Hart Donovan
1917-1918

By 1891, J.J. Donovan had finished his work with the Fairhaven Land Company. That year found him working many jobs. He became Chief Engineer for the Tideland Appraisers and Chief Engineer and Manager of the Bellingham Bay & Eastern Railway (BB&E). He was also the Chief Engineer and Manager of the Blue Canyon Mine at the south end of Lake Whatcom. He became one of the owners of the mine during this period along with Julius H. Bloedel. Bloedel and Donovan would forge a relationship of lasting importance. The third partner was Peter Larson, a wealthy railroad contractor and entrepreneur from Helena, Montana, who would finance several of Bloedel and Donovan's ventures.

Center for Pacific Northwest Studies, Western Washington University

Three partners: Bloedel, Donovan, and Larson.

Miners near the entrance to the Blue Canyon Mine.

The mine was started by Fairhaven speculator and banker Jim Wardner in 1889. He soon sold his interest and his associates, J.H. Bloedel, Donovan, Larson and others had taken charge. Coal was at first barged down the lake and delivered to the coal bunker on the bay by horse and wagon. In 1891 the Bellingham Bay and Eastern Railroad was formed to build the railroad along the north side of the lake to deliver the coal to the bunkers. J.J. Donovan became its chief engineer and general manager. That roadway is now the Ken Hertz Trail.

In 1898 the three partners formed the Lake Whatcom Logging Company and began logging the slopes around the lake.

As logging moved east, the BB&E track was extended up to Acme-Wickersham where it connected to the Northern Pacific. In 1902 the line was sold to the Northern Pacific.

Blue Canyon Coal Bunkers, 1892

The BB&E coal train is on the wharf unloading into the gravity bunkers. A large sailing ship is docked below taking on coal, probably bound for San Francisco. The high wharf was also used for dumping logs into the boom shown. The bunkers were located on Bellingham Bay just north of the border between Bellingham and Sehome. (Howard Buswell photograph)

BB&E Locomotive and Crew

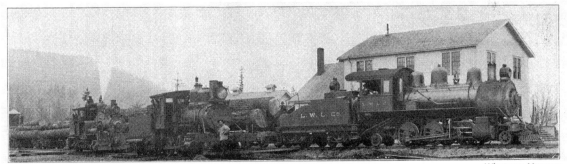

Lake Whatcom Logging Locomotives

The Lake Whatcom Logging Company first logged on the slopes around the lake and later, Saxon and Alger. Railroads were built to bring the logs to the lake where they could be gathered in booms and towed up the lake to the mill. Here are shown the company's Shay, Baldwin and American locomotives.

J.J. Donovan, J.H. Bloedel and Peter Larson had formed the Lake Whatcom Logging Company in 1898.

In July of 1901 the three partners decided to saw and sell their own lumber and they formed Larson Lumber Company. Larson, the primary investor was president, Bloedel was the manager, and Donovan was the logging manager. They bought land at the north end of the lake and built

Larson Mill, Lake Whatcom. Company workers' houses are seen outside the perimeter fence.

a large saw and shingle mill. The mill began cutting in 1901 and operated under several different ownerships until 1958.

The company eventually built two sawmills on this site. Mill A was a sawmill and shingle mill on the present site of Bloedel Donovan Park. Mill B, a saw mill and planing mill, adjoined it to the south on land that is now occupied by Old Mill Village.

Bellingham Bay & British Columbia Railroad Depot

In 1898, upon retirement of Mark L. Stangroom, J.J. Donovan was hired as General Superintendent and Chief Engineer of the BB&BC. It was Whatcom County's first railroad, and ran from the Sehome Dock at the foot of Cornwall Avenue to Sumas. The BB&BC established Railroad Avenue.

Its imposing Victorian passenger depot and hotel stood on the present site of Depot Market Square. The old depot was razed in 1942, and the property remained a parking lot until the present farmer's market site was constructed in 2007.

BB&BC Log Train

In 1883 the BB&BC was incorporated with the goal of connecting Bellingham Bay to the Canadian Pacific Railroad at Sumas. In later years the track was extended into the Nooksack River drainage system as far as Glacier, to serve the logging and mining activity there.

Donovan's dream of extending the line across the North Cascades to Spokane faded with the death of Pierre Cornwall. The line was sold in 1911 to the Milwaukee and St. Paul Railroad. Trains continued to operate on Railroad Avenue until 1980.

Peter Larson died in 1909. Julius Bloedel, J.J. Donovan, and the widowed Margaret Larson now owned the Lake Whatcom Logging Company and Larson Mill Company. They needed access to salt water transportation.

In 1913 Bloedel and Donovan formed Bloedel Donovan Lumber Mills and bought the Bellingham Bay Improvement Company Mill at the foot of Cornwall Avenue. They called it the Cargo Mill.

Bloedel Donovan Headquarters Building

This historic building built in 1917 still stands at the foot of Cornwall Avenue. The huge Cargo Mill built mostly on piling, extended down the shoreline behind this building for 2000 feet. In 2012, Nielsen Brothers Inc. remodeled the lower floor and built a new foundation, assuring the building's survival for future generations. Its upper floor now houses the office of its owners, Nielsen Brothers Inc. and the two lower floors are rental offices.

Bloedel Donovan Cargo Mill, 1928

An aerial photo shows the immensity of the Cargo Mill which in this year, 1928, was the world's largest producing sawmill. On the hill directly above the cylindrical waste burner, is St. Joseph's Hospital. Down the shoreline, south of the extensive log booms, can be seen the much smaller E.K. Wood Mill, now the site of Boulevard Park.

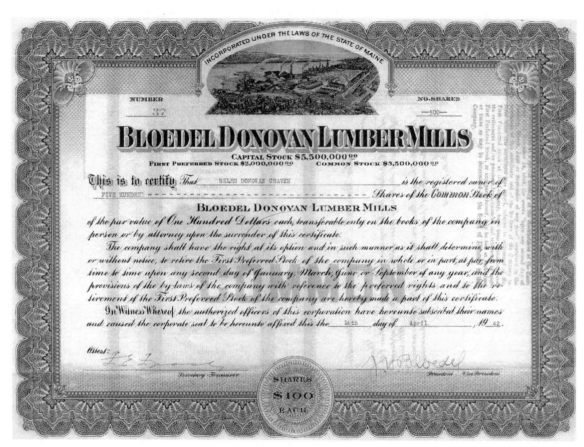

This stock certificate was one of several issued to J.J. Donovan's daughter, Helen Donovan Craven, and signed by J.H. Bloedel, President.

These huge stacks of lumber are air drying and waiting on the docks to be shipped. 'Sticks' separate each plank of lumber to allow air circulation and drying of the freshly cut wood.

The *Vigilant* sits at the Cargo Mill

The famed schooner *Vigilant* sits at the Cargo Mill dock waiting to be loaded. St. Joseph's Hospital is seen on the hill behind the steam and smoke from the mill. Built in 1919, by the George Matthews yard in Hoquiam, she was the last of a storied fleet of ships built by the E.K. Wood Company to carry lumber to Pacific ports. She operated out of Bellingham until 1940.

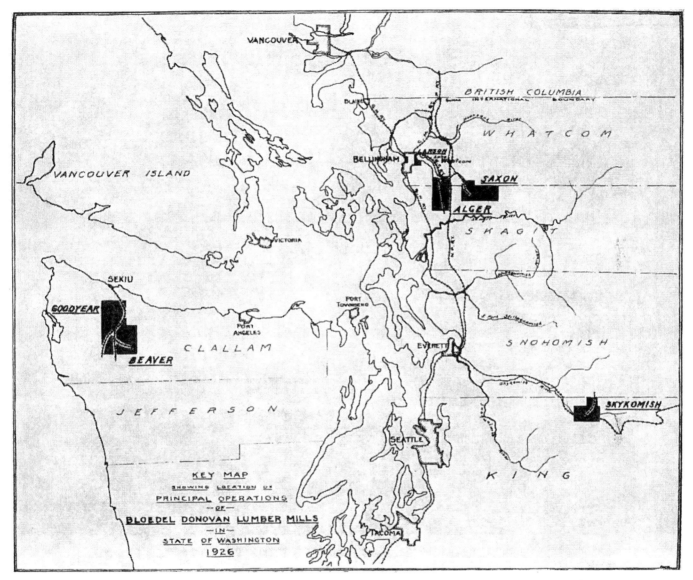

Treasures from the Trunk

Bloedel Donovan Lumber Mills conducted logging operations on huge acreages over a wide area. Logs were brought to the mills by rail or towed in rafts on the sea. Much of the transport was on the companies own logging railroads.

Whatcom Museum

LOGGING CAMP OF BLOEDEL DONOVAN LUMBER MILLS AT ALGER, WASH., AND TOWN ADJACENT WHERE MARRIED EMPLOYEES RESIDE.

Whatcom Museum

Bloedel Donovan, Alger Camp. The company attempted to stabilize their labor force by providing decent housing, housing for married men, and an early form of health insurance for workers. This was the camp at Alger and the town adjacent where married employees lived.

Whatcom Museum, Darius Kinsey photo

Skykomish Logging Bridge, 1923. This bridge, designed by J.N. Donovan across the Skykomish River, was but one of many bridges scattered over the 50 miles of railroad built and owned by the Company in the State of Washington.

Bloedel Donovan bought the Goodyear Lumber Company timber holdings in Clallam County in October 1923. From the booming grounds in Clallam Bay their operations spread south and east. New camps were established at Sappho, Beaver, Hoko and Pysht.

The Calawah camp seen here used portable bunkhouses designed by J.J. The combined operations employed 800 to 1000 men. The company built more than 100 miles of railroad and over 20 years harvested more than four billion feet of timber.

Whatcom Museum

Calawah Camp

Sekiu, Clallam Bay

The booming grounds at Sekiu were in the protected waters of Clallam Bay. Here logs were delivered by rail, dumped into the water and gathered into log booms to be towed to the BDLM's Cargo Mill on the Bellingham waterfront.

Saxon Camp

The Saxon camp east of Lake Whatcom featured J.J.'s portable camp buildings which could be moved from place to place by rail as the timber cut progressed.

Seeking a way to utilize lower grade lumber the company built this box factory on Cornwall Avenue across from the headquarters building. The factory opened in 1918. It proved far more profitable than expected and so when it burned in 1925, it was immediately rebuilt. Egg crates, fruit boxes and can cases were made. Hundreds of thousands of wooden cases were manufactured by Bloedel Donovan for military use during World War II.

Whatcom Museum, J.W. Sandison photo

The Box Factory

This Sandison photo shows J.J. Donovan and his son J.N. Donovan at their desks in the Bloedel Donovan headquarters building at the foot of Cornwall. J.J.'s Rotary Club emblem is displayed below the large photograph of a tree.

	1919	1920	1921	1922	1923	1924
Sales	$4,263,312.37	$6,097,675.90	$3,277,781.53	$4,692,413.76	$7,307,605.71	$5,752,113.00
Deduct						
Manufacturing Costs	2,914,010.02	4,331,206.95	2,551,255.74	3,622,900.99	5,302,437.19	4,260,806.31
Taxes including Federal	214,608.08	294,126.29	72,542.81	92,551.07	158,983.88	135,563.80
TOTAL	$3,128,618.10	$4,625,333.24	$2,623,798.55	$3,715,452.06	$5,461,421.07	$4,396,370.11
Gross profit before deducting depletion and depreciation	$1,134,694.27	$1,472,342.66	$ 653,982.98	$ 976,961.70	$1,846,184.64	$1,355,742.89
Add Miscellaneous Income	41,728.01	35,704.33	27,855.01	32,765.97	24,914.76	38,918.16
TOTAL	$1,176,422.28	$1,508,046.99	$ 681,837.99	$1,009,727.67	$1,871,099.40	$1,394,661.05
Deduct						
General expenses	$ 191,933.44	$ 308,530.36	$ 348,921.35	$ 493,833.00	$ 529,427.02	$ 517,773.49
Compensation of officers	35,600.00	29,666.67	28,000.00	28,000.00	30,000.00	35,000.00
TOTAL	$ 227,533.44	$ 338,197.03	$ 376,921.35	$ 521,833.00	$ 559,427.02	$ 552,773.49
Balance — being profit before deducting depletion, depreciation and interest	$ 948,888.84	$1,169,849.96	$ 304,916.64	$ 487,894.67	$1,311,672.38	$ 841,887.56
Deduct						
Depletion of timber	$ 255,959.67	$ 231,017.19	$ 110,764.89	$ 138,534.37	$ 430,356.22	$ 441,915.35
Depreciation	119,643.27	138,350.07	147,464.58	157,174.04	174,784.63	142,307.05
Interest	45,082.14	53,647.89	44,870.62	73,061.02	118,781.39	210,607.82
TOTAL	$ 420,685.08	$ 423,015.15	$ 303,100.09	$ 368,769.43	$ 723,922.24	$ 794,830.22
Balance — being net profit	$ 528,203.76	$ 746,834.81	$ 1,816.55	$ 119,125.24	$ 587,750.14	$ 47,057.34

Treasures from the Trunk

Bloedel Donovan Profit & Loss Statement

13½ YEARS ENDED JUNE 30, 1932

1925	1926	1927	1928	1929	1930	1931	6 Months 1932	Total 13½ Years
$5,966,289.21	$6,011,589.46	$7,224,947.22	$8,988,127.49	$9,374,961.75	$7,736,884.23	$4,212,295.91	$1,255,509.70	$82,161,507.24
4,606,175.12	4,072,762.85	4,721,118.77	6,600,250.10	7,024,531.98	6,436,645.87	3,894,504.57	1,086,435.31	61,425,041.77
95,227.56	91,966.22	179,445.79	238,374.52	252,598.96	174,146.25	155,959.21	75,300.00	2,231,394.44
$4,701,402.68	$4,164,729.07	$4,900,564.56	$6,838,624.62	$7,277,130.94	$6,610,792.12	$4,050,463.78	$1,161,735.31	$63,656,436.21
$1,264,886.53	$1,846,860.39	$2,324,382.66	$2,149,502.87	$2,097,830.81	$1,126,092.11	$ 161,832.13	$ 93,774.39	$18,505,071.03
65,371.44	66,102.55	149,484.90	117,151.03	171,823.34	62,110.86	143,644.42	44,730.73	1,022,305.51
$1,330,257.97	$1,912,962.94	$2,473,867.56	$2,266,653.90	$2,269,654.15	$1,188,202.97	$ 305,476.55	$ 138,505.12	$19,527,376.54
$ 531,063.60	$ 563,496.54	$ 693,728.64	$ 425,880.53	$ 454,450.45	$ 417,394.47	$ 293,014.84	$ 107,305.87	$ 5,876,753.60
35,728.00	36,000.00	38,000.00	38,000.00	37,508.34	43,100.00	40,235.86	20,522.50	475,361.37
$ 566,791.60	$ 599,496.54	$ 731,728.64	$ 463,880.53	$ 491,958.79	$ 460,494.47	$ 333,250.70	$ 127,828.37	$ 6,352,114.97
$ 763,466.37	$1,313,466.40	$1,742,138.92	$1,802,773.37	$1,777,695.36	$ 727,708.50	$ 27,774.15	$ 10,676.75	$13,175,261.57
$ 313,264.60	$ 445,010.98	$ 690,608.30	$ 663,034.74	$ 569,589.10	$ 532,575.79	$ 340,761.98	$ 151,033.40	$ 5,314,426.58
159,323.72	189,826.33	203,359.61	271,574.82	349,506.41	306,613.92	262,666.65	115,016.51	2,737,611.61
151,304.67	140,135.08	95,112.89	92,848.78	146,899.91	110,985.66	157,905.08	105,084.36	1,546,327.31
$ 623,892.99	$ 774,972.39	$ 989,080.80	$1,027,458.34	$1,065,995.42	$ 950,175.37	$ 761,333.71	$ 371,134.27	$ 9,598,365.50
$ 139,573.38	$ 538,494.01	$ 753,058.12	$ 775,315.03	$ 711,699.94	$ 222,466.87	$ 789,107.86	$ 360,457.52	$ 3,576,896.07

This interesting document reveals the financial record of the company for a 13.5-year period.
The Great Depression caused their first losing year, shown above in darker box.

Columbia Valley Lumber Company

The Columbia Valley Lumber Company was formed in 1913 to provide a retail outlet for BDLM products. The Bellingham store shown here was one of 13 retail lumberyards that the company operated in the state. A number of them were in eastern Washington. Earl Levalley, who had started with the company's Wenatchee yard, became the general manager in 1929.

Diamond B Fuel Company

In the beginning, scraps and mill ends were simply burned in the huge burners at lumber mills. Soon however, selling mill ends for heating fuel created an additional revenue source for mills. Bloedel Donovan established the Diamond B Fuel Company, taking its name from the Bloedel Donovan logo, a large B in a diamond shape. Diamond B sold and delivered mill ends to residences and businesses throughout the county to be used for heating.

The whole image is a Cirkut photo. The Cirkut is a rotating panoramic camera, of the type known as 'full rotation'. The photo nicely illustrates the transition from horse-drawn transportation to the automobile era.

Bloedel Donovan Lumber Mills went out of business in 1945. Their timber land in Washington had been exhausted. J.J. Donovan had died, and J.H. Bloedel had turned his attention to lumbering opportunities in British Columbia. The company sold off collateral operations like Columbia Valley Lumber Company and Diamond B. Fuel and closed it doors. The Cargo Mill was purchased by the Port of Bellingham in November 1947. To clear the site for possible re-use the Cargo Mill was deliberately burned in March 1950, and its smokestack toppled. It was the end of an era.

Whatcom Museum, Jack Carver photo

Whatcom Museum

Big Ole, an audible community icon, was a giant steam whistle mounted on the roof of the Bloedel Donovan Cargo Mill. It could be heard all over town announcing the beginning of work at 8 am, the noon hour, and quitting time at 5 pm. People set their watches by it. In the 1940s J.H. Bloedel moved the great whistle to his mill in Port Alberni, British Columbia, and Bellingham mourned. In 2001 when the Port Alberni mill closed, Todd Warger of the Whatcom Museum succeeded in bringing it back to Bellingham. Big Ole lives again on the roof of the Western Washington University steam plant, where it serves as the campus emergency alarm.

Bloedel Donovan Park

The Bloedel family gave the site of the former Larson Mill A to the City of Bellingham to be used as a park. Julius Bloedel is seen here at the dedication ceremonies on August 11, 1948. Seated to the right in the front row, hat in hand, is Jack Donovan, representing the Donovan family in the dedication.

The other Larson sawmill, Mill B, continued to be used by Columbia Valley Lumber Company until it burned in 1958. The planing mill was used by Robinson Plywood & Lumber Company until the mid-1960s. The land is now occupied by Old Mill Village.

Community Man

John Joseph Donovan was a man of vast energies and many interests. His community activities were so numerous that it is difficult to imagine how he could have balanced the heavy duties of his business career and still devote so much time to civic, cultural and religious affairs.

He served on the City Council of Fairhaven for two terms, he helped to get St. Joseph's Hospital operating, he served for eight years on the Board of Trustees of the Normal School, and he sat as president of several cultural and professional associations.

Whatcom Museum

The Main Building of the State Normal School at Bellingham in 1901, now Western Washington University.

In 1912 Donovan constructed this building at Holly and Commercial Street. It was designed by F. Stanley Piper and occupied by Wahl's Department Store, Bellingham's premier dry goods store. It also housed the Grand Theater.

J.J. sold it on contract to J.B. Wahl shortly after it was completed, but not before he could exercise his sense of moral indignation at the kind of shows the Grand Theater was running. The building was demolished when National Bank of Commerce built the large bank now on that half block.

Whatcom Museum

The Donovan Building on W. Holly Street

**Grand Theater Opening
Announcement**

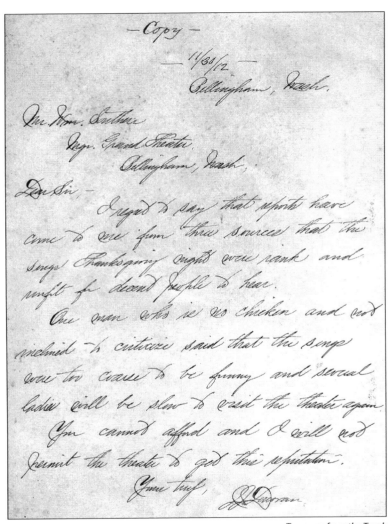

Treasures from the Trunk

J.J. as censor. This amusing letter written to his tenant, the Grand Theater operator, criticizes a performance at the theater. Donovan had strong moral convictions.

Whatcom Museum

Donovan was a devout Catholic, and he was a dedicated supporter of Catholic causes. He helped raise the funds to build Assumption Church on Cornwall Avenue, and he donated the cross on its tower.

J.J. Donovan is seen behind the clergy to the right of the group.

Assumption Catholic Church, Cornwall Avenue

In the 1920s, the Ku Klux Klan was influential in the Pacific Northwest. It maintained a strong presence in Bellingham for a number of years to the concern and consternation of many. In 1926, they sought to enter a float in the annual Tulip Festival Parade. J.J. Donovan was chair of the parade committee that year. He denied them entry. They countered by holding their own parade one week later.

Whatcom Museum

The Tulip Festival Parade

The traditional Bellingham parade route came down Cornwall Avenue past the Assumption Church. The Klan parade followed that route a week later being sure to offend and threaten the Catholics, one of the minorities whom they vilified.

J.J. Donovan was a committed foe of the Klan. In a rousing address in 1923 he flayed the invisible empire, which merited this headline in the Seattle Daily Times.

The text of J.J.'s remarks:

"There are forces at work which seek to spread discord in this community by appeals to religious bigotry, to race hatred and to lust for political power. The most sinister of these forces is the Ku Klux Klan. Claiming to enforce law, it commits the most dastardly outrages, including murder. In the name of religion it proscribes Catholics and Jews and undertakes to see that

Seattle Daily Times, July 25, 1923. Treasures from the Trunk

Whatcom Museum

KKK pamphlet

they hold no office and teach no school. Boasting of patriotism, it is a traitor to the fundamental principles of the constitution, hiding behind masks, striking in the dark, it is a monster so hideous that no honest man can continue in its rank.

"No calumny is too foul. No oath nor statements too obscene for its propaganda. The great magazine, World's Work well describes the organization as 'salesmen of hate'. Read the series of articles begun in May in that magazine if you would know more of the vileness of this organization, the character of its leaders, and its real object which is to obtain $16.54 in exchange for $2.00 worth of cotton cloth. A meaningless jargon of idiotic titles and pamphlets filled with lies seeking to stir up hatred."

"I would not dignify this collection of rogues and fools with such attention were it not that they openly boast that having captured our neighbor state of Oregon they will now control Washington. They will find here, men of different breed."

—J.J. Donovan, Seattle Daily Times

This Ku Klux Klan robe and hood were found in a house on York Street and were placed in the collection of the Whatcom Museum. This chilling reminder of the bigotry of an earlier age is shown to illustrate the courage and character of J.J. Donovan who was an outspoken foe of this organization of hatred and violence.

For State Senator

Bellingham City District

42ND

A Vote For **Kline**

Is FOR the Saloons

A Vote For **Donovan**

Is AGAINST the Saloons

A Vote For **Other Candidates**

Is THROWN AWAY

S. B. Irish & Co., Printing Bellingham, Washington

Treasures from the Trunk

J.J. Donovan's lifelong interest in community affairs prompted him to serve two terms on Fairhaven's first city councils in the 1890s. Consumed with business affairs he turned down many entreaties to run for public office. He was urged to run for Mayor of Bellingham in 1901 and in subsequent years. In 1910, he responded to his moral beliefs and ran for the Washington State Senate. His opponent represented the tavern interests while J.J. stood for "Temperance and Moderation". He lost the election.

Washington Good Roads Association

For many years Donovan joined Sam Hill struggling for good roads for the State of Washington. In 1916, Chuckanut Drive was opened. Prior to that, access to Bellingham was possible only by rail or boat. Donovan was a member of 'The Old Guard' of this association who fought long and hard for good roads. J.J. stands in the front row left.

The Washington Club, 1928

This jovial group of men met monthly to trade insults and humor in a long tradition that lasted until the 1980s. This photo was taken at the Bloedel Donovan Logging camp in Alger. J.J. kneels in the front row center with a youngster on his knee, perhaps his granddaughter Patricia.

The Washington Club at The Bellingham Hotel

This photo shows the club's bronze bull, emblematic of their primary function. J.J. stands in the gutter wearing a fireman's hat. Noted Fairhaven humorist, George Finnegan, stands just behind J.J. wearing a volunteer fireman's cap. This organization was all about laughter and fun.

The Rotary Club Of Bellingham, 1926

Most of the elite of Bellingham business and society are represented in this photo taken in front of the Leopold Hotel. J.J. was a committed Rotarian and served as the club's president in 1928. Here he is seen in the back row, barely visible, not his accustomed position in photographs.

Number Please! Donovan's prominent position in Bellingham's business and society made him a natural for publicity of any kind. Here he is shown celebrating the 50th anniversary of the telephone in a telephone company promotion.

The Purdy Party, April 12, 1924

J.J. Donovan was Vice President of 'Mr Purdy's Bank', the Bellingham 1st National Bank. He and Clara threw a party for Mildred Purdy, the daughter of E.W. Purdy and Marcella Purdy. Marcella is front center in the picture surrounded by (L to R): Mrs Victor Roth, Clara Donovan, Mrs Purcell, Mrs Harold Lowery, Hazel Donovan, Mrs W.C. Carver and Mrs Arynnes Bolster.

Courtesy "Worcester Evening Post"

Now They Wear Doctors' Hoods
A. D. Flinn, '93, J. J. Donovan, '82, G. W. Patterson, '88, President Earle,
Dr. Knapp, L. P. Alford, '96

Worcester Polytechnic Institute Library, Special Collections.

Worcester Polytechnic Institute, Honorary Doctorate, 1932

J.J. Donovan was invited to give the commencement address at his alma-mater. He was given an honorary Doctorate in Engineering. It was surely one of the high moments of his life. It also marked the beginning of the end. His daughter Helen, who attended the event, reported later that in the midst of his address he stopped, confused for a moment and then recovered to finish his usual robust delivery. It was the first revelation of the dementia that would eventually claim him.

Whatcom Museum

"The Flight of the Years"
~ 1858 - 75 - 82 - 87 - 88 - 92 ~

Robed in white a baby lay,
    Blue-eyed, laughing, long ago,
Smiling, cooing, all the day
    Though the world was deep in snow,
        And the wintry sun rose late,
        When she came in Fifty-eight.

Clad in blue, a graceful girl
    Speaks the words that sweetly tell
Of the coming of God's pearl,
    His child-angel, Baby Bell,
        And with sympathies alive
        My heart's hers in Seventy-five.

Bright the glow on western sky,
    Hot the words my lips are saying,
For I love you, though I die
    And the hour is past for playing.
        Time has come to dare and do,
        'Westward Ho' in Eighty-two.

Five long years on western plain,
    Then again I see my queen,
And the longing and the pain
    End at last in bliss supreme.
        We are very near to heaven,
        Heart to heart in Eighty-seven.

John Joseph Donovan possessed boundless energy. Highly intelligent, he was an organized, detail-minded engineer but also a passionate and emotional Irishman. His love letters to his Nickie were warm and moving.

His poetry was skillful and fetching. *The Flight of the Years* was written for their fifth anniversary. It is a touching review of their lives, their love and his prayer for the future: "helpers, lovers, still to be, unto the end, eternity."

SIDE BY SIDE AND EYE TO EYE,
  WITH THE ROSES ON YOUR BREAST,
PLEDGING LOVE UNTIL WE DIE
  ASKING GOD FOR ALL THAT'S BEST,
  LIFE'S COMPLETE AND HAPPY FATE
  WHEN WE WED IN EIGHTY-EIGHT.

FOUR YEARS MORE AND CHILDREN DEAR,
  BLESS OUR HOME, ENRICH oUR LIFE,
HELEN'S KISS DRIES UP A TEAR
  BRINGS THEE SUNSHINE, SWEETHEART, WIFE,
  WHILE OUR 'OSEBUD'S GURGLING COO
  WARMS THY HEART IN NINETY-TWO.

SO, MAYOURNEEN, LIFE GOES ON
  AND THE YEARS ARE BUT A DAY.
DUTIES NEW ARE LAID UPON
  BOTH OUR SHOULDERS. LET US PRAY
  HELPERS, LOVERS, STILL TO BE
  UNTO THE END, ETERNITY.

April 29th,
~ 1892 ~

VOL. XXXIV — NO. 3.

J. J. DONOVAN GREAT BUILDER OF WEST, DIES

Distinguished N.W. Leader's Career Ends

Thousands Honor Memory —Bishop Shaughnessy Presides At Funeral Mass

J. J. Donovan of Bellingham, one of the West's great builders, and honored by thousands as a man of faith, a man of honor and sterling worth, was called to his eternal reward last Saturday. Death came to him in his Garden street home, where members of the immediate family were at his bedside. He was 78 years of age.

The funeral Mass was offered in Assumption Church, Bellingham on Tuesday morning. His Excellency the Most Reverend Gerald Shaughnessy, S. M., Bishop of Seattle presided in the sanctuary. The Right Rev. Monsignor Stafford, pastor, was celebrant of the requiem Mass and preached the sermon.

For his text, Monsignor Stafford selected: "He that eateth My flesh and drinketh My blood hath everlasting life, and I will raise him up on the last day." St. John VI-55.

His Spiritual Life Key To Greatness

Developing the idea of life — natural and supernatural life and the Eucharistic life, Monsignor Stafford recalled Mr. Donovan's deep devotion to the Holy Eucharist and said that his highly cultivated spiritual life was the key to his great achievements as well as to the noble character for

J. J. DONOVAN, of Bellingham, who died last Saturday, is mourned throughout the Northwest as one of the greatest civic leaders of the state.

CHARITIES CONCLAVE AIDS ENROLLMENT AT MARYKNOLL SCHOOL

Far reaching effects of the National Conference of Catholic Charities which was held in Seattle last August include the present enrollment of 50 new Japanese pupils at Maryknoll School, it has just been announced. Pres-

EMP MAS U.S.

Split In Diff L

WASH

(By N. WASHI employmen of the new fundament the proble the Admin contend in

Upon it, cated in h balancing tailment of removal o recovery. found of p the severa who now h wages whic sustaining, over which being furro

As Congr the situatio have to dea

The Pr served noti if it does the unemp tinue.

Labor pr controlling thirty-hour corporation minimum maximum

The Catholic Northwest Progress newspaper wrote of Donovan's death in a long article reciting the high points of his life and his steadfast and lifelong devotion to his faith and ending with the words, "May his soul have rest eternal."

Treasures from the Trunk

J. J. Donovan died on January 27, 1937. The Bellingham Herald announced his passage with this front page headline. His death was reported in many newspapers of the day, including the New York Times, for J.J.'s influence had spread far beyond the confines of Bellingham Bay.

Whatcom Museum

Family Album

The trunk was filled with family photos, hundreds and hundreds of them, both in print and negative form. There were also six cans of 16-mm home movies taken by J.J. between 1924 and 1929. 31 minutes of movie film have been saved and digitized, and the exhibition includes a seven-minute narrated presentation of the best of those films.

Following are just a few of the family pictures of the Donovans selected to show in the exhibition.

Treasures from the Trunk, c.1914.

J.J. and Clara are sitting on a beach log with their new daughter-in-law, Geraldine Goodheart Donovan.

J.J. and his Sisters

J.J. Donovan took frequent business trips to the East Coast and always tried to find time for a visit with family in New Hampshire. Here he is with his four sisters. Kate stands at his left. The young girl is unidentified. None of the Donovan sisters had children.

Treasures from the Trunk

Katherine 'Kate' Donovan 1860–1951

Kate was the second child of Patrick and Julia Donovan. She was J.J.'s faithful sister and lifelong correspondent. Upon the death of their mother, Julia, Kate took on the role of housewife caring for 'Father' and the farm until his death. In J.J.'s words, "Kate sacrificed her youth to care for the family." She died a spinster in Plymouth at the age of 91.

On July 31, 1896, J.J.'s three younger sisters had their picture taken in Berlin, NH. The event is described in a letter from 'Maggie' to her brother. They are Julia Teresa, Margaret, and Mary Agnes. Unfortunately we cannot assign names to faces.

Treasures from the Trunk

Julia Teresa Donovan (Tot) came to Bellingham for a visit in the spring of 1926. She stopped off in Chicago for a visit with her niece, Helen Donovan Craven. Here she is with grand nieces, Elizabeth and Frances Craven. J.J. wrote on the back of the snapshot, "My sister Julia & Helen's children, May 1926."

Whatcom Museum

Clara Nichols Donovan, 1858–1936

Clara I. Nichols was born in Haverhill, NH. A graduate of the Plymouth Normal School, she taught in one-room school houses for three years before turning to her true love, music. She taught private piano for six years in Melrose, MA, and then married J.J. Donovan and moved with him to Fairhaven in 1888.

John Joseph Donovan, 1858–1937

Whatcom Museum

Helen Donovan Craven, 1889–1958. Helen Donovan was the first child of J.J. and Clara Donovan. In 1921 she married Leslie Craven who had grown up across the street. They had three children: Elizabeth Page Craven, Frances Louise Craven and Donovan Craven. They lived in Evanston, Illinois.

Treasures from the Trunk

Leslie Craven, 1887–1985. Leslie Craven was raised in Bellingham, the son of Arthur J. Craven a prominent local attorney and Emily K. Craven. He graduated from Stanford University and attended Harvard and Stanford Law Schools. He became a nationally known attorney specializing in railroad law. As a youth he lived with his parents at 1120 Garden Street, just a few houses away from the Donovan home at 1201 Garden Street.

Whatcom Museum

Geraldine Goodheart Donovan, 1892–1975

Geraldine, daughter of Dr. & Mrs John Goodheart, married John N. Donovan. The Russian wolfhound, 'Yaransk of Tatiana' is seen in many pictures.

J.N. 'Jack' Donovan succeeded his father as Vice President of Bloedel Donovan Lumber Mills and was an engineering graduate of Worcester Polytechnic University. He married Geraldine Goodheart. They had two surviving children, Patricia Donovan Cunningham Plym and John Joseph Donovan II. Their first child, John Nichols Donovan Jr. 'Baby Jack', died in a tragic auto accident at age 3.

Treasures from the Trunk

John Nichols Donovan, 1891–1961

Treasures from the Trunk

Young J.N. 'Jack' Donovan with dog.

Don't you know I came early this year,

just to wish you a

A Merrie Christmas

and a

Happy New Year

John Nichols Donovan, Jr.

Whatcom Museum, gift of Gordon Tweit

Infant John Nichols Donovan Jr.

Philip Donovan and Hazel Prigmore were married in 1916. The groom is standing third from the left behind the bride. Other members of the wedding party are not identified.

Hazel Prigmore Donovan, 1893–1989. Hazel was the wife of Philip Donovan. She is pictured here with her sons, Robert 'Bobbie' and Arnold Matier Donovan.

Phil Donovan was a graduate of Worcester Polytechnic University. He was for a time employed by Bloedel Donovan Lumber Mills before becoming an automobile dealer. He and a partner owned the Lasalle, Cadillac agency which was located in the building now housing the Community Food Co-op. Later he was an owner of Northwest Fuel Company. He married Hazel Hart Prigmore. Their children were Philip Hart Donovan who died as an infant, Robert W. Donovan, Carol Donovan, and adopted son Arnold Matier Donovan.

Whatcom Museum

Philip Laurence Donovan, 1893-1961

Whatcom Museum

At the country club. L to R: 2 unknown friends, Phil, Geraldine, Jack, Hazel, Clara and two unidentified men, and Arnold. On bench Patricia, J.J., John and Bobbie.

Treasures from the Trunk

J.J. with first grandchild, 'Baby Jack' who died so tragically within the year.

This battered toy locomotive is the surviving piece of the magnificent Buddy-L train set given by J.J. Donovan to his grandson J.J. Donovan II.

The train set complete with track and trestle is seen on the wall behind the J.N. Donovan home (444 15th Street), being admired by young John, his sister Patricia (2nd from left), and two unidentified friends. The toy railroad was set up on the grounds of the 15th Street home and played with for years by John and his friends.

This 1923 photo of their home shows Clara Donovan's Detroit Electric automobile parked in front. Electric automobiles were popular among wealthy ladies in the 1920s because they could be started by the flick of a switch. Gasoline automobiles were started with a hand crank requiring more strength and daring.

Patricia, age 2, with the Detroit Electric auto in background.

This grand house at 1201 N. Garden Street became the home of the Donovans in 1905. It was built in 1890 by Edward and Bertha Fischer. Bertha was the daughter of Pierre Cornwall. The house is on the National Historic Register. It is now owned by Daniel J. Hovorka, DMD, who has his dental practice on the ground floor. The upper floors are rented rooms.

'Jack' and Geraldine Donovan built this home at the corner of Garden and 15th Streets in 1924. The house still stands at 444 15th Street, now surrounded by a large hedge.

J.J. & Friends at Mt Baker

This snapshot was taken by local engineer/photographer Bert Huntoon, while on a hike in the snow. Table Mountain is in the background. It looks as if J.J. is about to fling a snowball at the cameraman.

Objects Displayed in the Exhibition

Treasures from the Trunk

John Joseph Donovan began writing diaries in 1872 when he was 13 years old. He continued the practice all of his life. Forty-two of his diaries survived among the *Treasures from the Trunk*. In them he chronicles growing up on a farm in New Hampshire, his mother's death, the joys and sorrows of his long romance with Clara, riding stagecoaches in the West, and the high moments of his adventurous life. They are a true historical treasure. The stain on the corner of this diary is explained in his May 9, 1883 entry, "This book was in my 'war bag' with a bottle of Sozodont, result can be seen on lower corners of each page." (Sozodont was a teeth cleaner and dental hygiene product popular in the late 1800s.)

Treasures from the Trunk

The Donovans were prolific letter writers. Before telephones, typewriters or email, hand-written letters were the means of communication, and the Donovans seemed to have saved them all. 2,047 letters in their envelopes were found in the trunk. The first were written in 1872. They provide an intimate view of the private lives of the Donovan family. These letters have all been read, organized chronologically and bundled by year. Hundreds, perhaps thousands, of business letters also were found in the trunk with letterheads from scores of early businesses.

Henck's Field Book. J.J.'s diary entry of February 1, 1881 states, "this morning I bought Henck's Fieldbook." J.J. was an engineering student at Worcester Polytechnic Institute. The book was found in the trunk 132 years later.

Railroad Passes

There were hundreds of railroads in the United States in Donovan's day. The custom was to send courtesy passes to the executives of other friendly railroads. J.J. had scores of free passes in 1905 when he was the General Superintendent of the Bellingham Bay and British Columbia Railroad. This collection found in his trunk illustrates the variety.

Patek Philippe Gold Watch

When Philip Donovan graduated from Worcester Polytechnic Institute in 1915, his proud father presented him with one of the worlds finest pocket watches. This Patek Phillipe gold watch is engraved with Philip's name and his date of graduation.

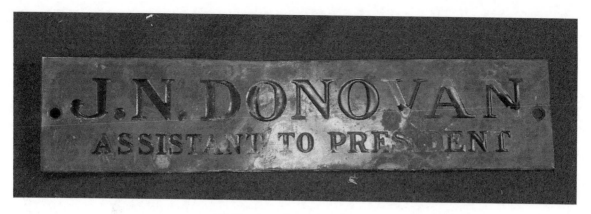

J.N. Donovan Brass Nameplate

Printed piece of lumber, printed in black and red.

Loaned by Nielsen Brothers Inc.

The objects on these two pages were found during the 2012 remodeling of the Bloedel Donovan Headquarters building. The owners, Nielsen Brothers Inc., found the brass nameplate of J.N. Donovan, bent and corroded, in the crawlspace under the building.

The time cards and wooden packaging brace were found in the floor joists between floors. The timecards indicate the working hours on December 31, 1936, for Nils Anderson, John DeLong and Gordon Leal.

Time Cards

The Bellingham Bay and British Columbia Railroad was sold in 1912 to the Milwaukee Road. J.J. Donovan had been its General Superintendent and Chief Engineer since 1898. The Railroad's San Francisco owners presented Donovan with a magnificent mahogany chest bound with silver containing twelve complete place settings of ornate sterling silver dinnerware. The China is Limoges. A place setting and several serving pieces are displayed at the exhibition and are pictured here.

These large and lovely sterling silver serving pieces were part of the presentation silver given to J.J. Donovan upon his retirement as General Superintendent of the Bellingham Bay and British Columbia Railroad. Their thanks for a job well done.

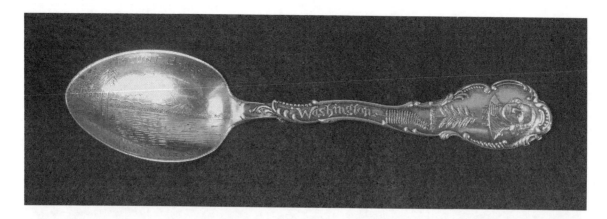

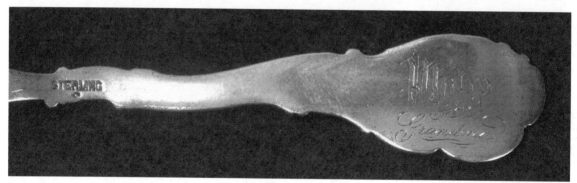

Philip's Baby Spoon

This sterling silver baby spoon is a souvenir spoon celebrating Washington achieving statehood in 1889. It was given to baby Philip Donovan, born in 1893, by his maternal grandmother Elizabeth Page Nichols. it is engraved "Philip from Grandma". Mrs. Nichols lived with the Donovans until her death. She is buried in Bayview Cemetery, Bellingham.

Books and Book Plates

J.J. and Clara Donovan were cultured, sophisticated and well-read people. In a letter to daughter Helen in the early 1930s Clara recites that a friend was organizing the books in their library for them. She had counted 3,400 books. Each book would have been adorned with this charming book plate. It depicts the side garden of their home at 1201 Garden Street. The garden gate is still there beside the house. The lovely image was drawn and signed by Elizabeth Colborne in 1925.

J.J. Donovan was an early adopter of technology. At every step of his life he was ready to embrace and adopt the latest inventions and put them to productive use.

He was a visionary, an innovator, a leader in business, church and community. Bellingham of the present owes much to the creativity that Donovan exercised in the past.

Treasures from the Trunk

The Eastman Kodak Co. began the home movie era in 1923 when they launched their 16-mm Cine-Kodak cameras and projector. J..J. owned a 1924 model like the camera shown and enjoyed taking movies of his family and the trips he and Clara took. Thirty minutes of his home movies stored in these cans were found among the trunk items. The footage has been digitized and preserved. Seven minutes of film have been edited and narrated for showing at the *Treasures from the Trunk* exhibition.

Whatcom Museum

This small bottle was one of several bottles found at the site of the first St. Joseph's hospital on 17th street. The old hospital has been gone since 1900, but the occupants of the residence at 518 17th street keep finding old bottles as they dig in their flower beds. Hamlin's Wizard Oil was a patent medicine advertised as a cure-all remedy: "There is no sore it will not cure, no pain it will not ease". Of course, its contents were 70% alcohol.

Loaned by Dr. Dag Jensen

Hamlin's Wizard Oil

Notice to historians and researchers:
The contents of 'The Trunk' described in this catalog will be available for research at the Center for Pacific Northwest Studies, a unit of the Division of Heritage Resources, Goltz-Murray Archives Building, Western Washington University, 808 25th Street, Bellingham Washington, 98225-7747
ph: 360-650-7747
email: cpnws@wwu.edu

Made in the USA
San Bernardino, CA
23 October 2018